P9-AQD-992

Classroom Literature Circles
A Practical, Easy Guide

Grades 3 - 5

by Elizabeth Suarez Aguerre

Carson-Dellosa Publishing Company, Inc.

Greensboro, North Carolina.

Credits

Editor
Kelly Gunzenhauser

Layout Design
Jon Nawrocik

Illustrations
Bill Neville

Cover Design
Matthew Van Zomeren

Cover Photographs
© RubberBall Productions
Photo credit © Comstock, Inc.,
© 1999 EyeWire, Inc. All rights reserved.

© 2003, Carson-Dellosa Publishing Company, Inc., Greensboro, North Carolina 27425. The purchase of this material entitles the buyer to reproduce worksheets and activities for classroom use only—not for commercial resale. Reproduction of these materials for an entire school or district is prohibited. No part of this book may be reproduced (except as noted above), stored in a retrieval system, or transmitted in any form or by any means (mechanically, electronically, recording, etc.) without the prior written consent of Carson-Dellosa Publishing Co., Inc.

Printed in the USA • All rights reserved.   **ISBN 0-88724-944-2**

Special thanks go to . . .

Roxanne Rios, colleague and friend,
For starting the "adventure" of literature circles with me . . .

And to Pablo Aguerre, for truly believing this is "only the beginning."

Table of Contents

Literature Circles:
What are they and why should teachers use them?

What are literature circles?

Literature circles have been defined as a "strategy for," an "approach to," and a "method of " teaching literature. Regardless of the terms used, literature circles, quite simply, are small groups of students who read the same book and gather on a regular basis to discuss their reading. The purpose of literature circles, then, is to have students discuss, respond to, and think about real literature.

Literature circles can be incorporated into an existing reading program with minimal effort and maximum benefits. Your job is to set up the classroom literature circles system and to ensure that students are discussing the critical elements of the story and *thinking* about the literature. The great thing about literature circles is this: you still direct students and keep them focused so that they end up right where you want them, but the *students* do the thinking, writing, discussing, debating, and sharing. This book details the general how-to on introducing and implementing a literature circle system in a third- through fifth-grade classroom, provides the reproducible student role forms for literature circle activities, and offers strategies and additional reproducibles for specific situations.

This Chapter Includes:

* a description of the literature circles method

* an introduction to the roles

* a description and scenario of a literature circles classroom

* information about why literature circles are an effective way for students to study literature

Who can use literature circles?

Literature circles work at almost any grade level, but are most successful when used with students who are at least in third grade, after students are ready to independently tackle reading assignments beyond basal readers. The roles students play in their groups can be adapted to many skill levels. Additionally, literature circles can be incorporated easily into almost any existing reading program, because they are simply another, more effective way for students to discuss and appreciate literature.

What are the major components of literature circles?

The major components are the books, the role forms, and students. Literature circle discussions are based on reading assignments. Each student is assigned a role form to complete after the day's reading. The student then uses the completed form as a guide during the after-reading discussion. These role forms help students think about and discuss critical literary elements such as characters, vocabulary, etc., and can also be used to assess reading comprehension. There are several versions of each role form, so you can easily match the particular forms for each role to each student's level.

What are the student roles covered in this book?

 Circle Supervisor—guides the group throughout the literature circle discussion and ensures that the group work runs smoothly

 Story Summarizer—summarizes the day's reading and reviews it in the group discussion

 Question Creator—creates and answers questions that go along with the day's reading

 Imaginative Illustrator—visualizes and illustrates a scene from the day's reading, then shares it with the group members

 Word Watcher—identifies and defines critical vocabulary from the day's reading

 Bridge Builder—makes connections between events in the story and personal events

* A detailed description of each role is included in Chapter 2 (starting on page 10)

What does a literature circles classroom look like?

Without seeing literature circles in action, it can be difficult to understand how it all comes together. This section will help you really "get it." There are three chunks of time spent during a session: reading and role form completion time, group discussion time, and whole class discussion time. The following is a description of what literature circles would look like in a classroom in which students have learned the system.

The fourth-grade students in Mrs. Aguerre's classroom have been reading *There's a Boy in the Girls' Bathroom* by Louis Sachar (Random House, 1988). Mrs. Aguerre announces, "Today's circles will be based on chapters 14 through 17." To ensure that students know their literature circle roles for the day, she refers to the literature circles pocket chart, which is labeled with the names of the roles. Students' names are on index cards that rotate from pocket to pocket.

After answering any questions, Mrs. Aguerre sits at her desk and reads the day's chapters silently while students independently do the same. (Mrs. Aguerre usually reads the entire book before starting the literature circles unit, and then completes the reading a second time along with the students. She knows that doing her own reading models reading for the students.)

After several minutes, a handful of students finish the reading and role forms early, so each student collects his materials (book, completed role form, pencil, and often a highlighter or sticky notes) and sits in his designated group meeting spot. As these "early birds" wait for the rest of their literature circle members to assemble, they either add to their role forms; reread the day's chapters and highlight interesting words, phrases, etc.; read the next chapter independently; or complete Early Bird worksheets (pages 73-76).

When students are finished with the reading and filling out the role forms, the literature circle groups sit together with their materials. Each group's Circle Supervisor, whose responsibility is to keep order, leads the group members in taking turns reviewing and discussing the role forms. The real purpose of the role forms is to spark discussions and debates about the literature, so most of the time students are not even looking at their forms. Fortunately, Mrs. Aguerre's class has been doing literature circles for a few weeks now, and the Circle Supervisors' jobs are minimal.

During the discussion, Mrs. Aguerre walks around and joins different group discussions. She sees one group debating about why a character did something. These students are flipping through their books looking for a particular scene, and half of the group members disagree with the others as to the cause of the character's actions. The Circle Supervisor reminds her classmates to take turns while they attempt to convince each other. Mrs. Aguerre moves on to observe another group in which students are sharing the different ways in which a particular event in the day's reading reminded them of events from their own lives.

After a few more minutes, Mrs. Aguerre calls time, and students return to the whole-class setting. A few students share their thoughts and experiences on the day's literature circles. Mrs. Aguerre holds another question-and-answer session, and assigns a Group Assessment worksheet (page 57) for students to use to evaluate how well their group discussions went.

So . . . why should teachers use literature circles?

The previous scene shows what literature circles look like in action, but why should you bother using this particular approach to teach literature reading and critical thinking? There is a great deal of research to support the use of literature circles, and many teachers have seen the positive outcomes of using this method.

Researchers have found that the use of literature circles:
- allows students "to practice authentic reading behaviors," and sparks student interest through peer enthusiasm (Hollingsworth, 1998)
- invites students to actively participate in sharing their ideas and building meaning from what they read (Daniels, 1994)
- dramatically changes students' attitudes towards books and reading (Samway, Whang, Cade, et al. 1991)
- engages reluctant readers and helps them feel more confident (Samway, Whang, Cade, et al. 1991, Samway and Whang, 1996)
- increases "talk" about books both in and out of the classroom (Samway, Whang, Cade, et al. 1991)
- helps students understand themselves and others through personal connections made with characters and story themes (Samway, Whang, Cade, et al. 1991)

Teachers have found that the use of literature circles increases:
- the number of books read by students
- the time students spend reading on a nightly basis
- student interest in reading
- student awareness of reading strategies
- student selection of "high-quality" literature
- the amount of time spent "on task" during the reading block
- the completion rate of class work
- enthusiasm for learning

All about Roles and Role Forms

Other than books and students, roles are the critical components of literature circles. You must teach this information thoroughly, because the student role forms serve as the guide for the circle discussions. There are basic, critical elements students need to cover (such as characters, vocabulary, etc.) when responding to literature, but the possibilities for role forms are endless. Chapter 2 consists mainly of student role forms you can select and reproduce to make your job easier. The main purpose of the role forms is to have students respond and interact with the literature. Of course, students must first be taught how to complete and use the role forms within their literature circles. Once students know how to use the role forms, there is not much left for you to do except participate, observe, and assess.

Role Form Objectives:
- serve as the guide for circle discussions
- assess students' understanding of literature
- help students develop and use reading strategies
- encourage students to respond to and interact with literature

This Chapter Includes:

Reproducible role forms for each role. There are five roles plus a supervisor.

- Story Summarizer
- Question Creator
- Imaginative Illustrator
- Word Watcher
- Bridge Builder
- Circle Supervisor

Each role has various forms from which to select. For example, there are five forms for the role of Story Summarizer, so your task is to select the form that best suits each student's needs and abilities. These forms vary as to how complicated they are and how much time they take for students to complete. Therefore, there are harder forms for advanced students, and easier forms for students who take longer to finish the reading or need help to complete their work.

In addition to the five main roles, there is a role form for the Circle Supervisor (this role is performed simultaneously with another role). This role form does not require the student to respond in writing. Instead, this role form provides the Circle Supervisor with guidelines and reminders of how to keep other students engaged and active while in the literature circles.

(5 Forms)

The Story Summarizer's job is to summarize the day's reading. Students can summarize the reading using a "Fast Write," or a "Somebody-Wanted-But-So Then" chart. Students can retell story events by writing paragraphs, creating story maps, or drawing illustrations. These are all general reading strategies that can be used to reinforce the skill of summarizing. In order to create a unique Story Summarizer role form, use the reproducibles in this book as a guide.

A "Fast Write" (#1 of 5, page 17) is a literacy strategy found in several different writing strategy books, under different names. The student writes for five to ten minutes, focusing on content instead of spelling, grammar, etc. It is written "note-style," and is then used as a guide while the Story Summarizer retells the day's reading.

A "Somebody-Wanted-But-So Then" chart (#2 of 5, page 18) guides the student to summarize the story by filling in the Character(s), Goal, Problem, and Solution.

#3 of 5 (page 19) requires that the student summarize the reading in paragraph form.

#4 of 5 (page 20) has the student fill in a story map, which includes sections titled Character(s), Setting, Main events in order, Problem(s) the main character is facing, and Possible solution(s).

#5 of 5 (page 21) is simpler and may be more appropriate for a struggling or younger reader. It requires the student to summarize the reading in an illustration. Then, the student fills in blanks to tell what happened first, next, and last.

When the Story Summarizer shares in the literature circle, she should retell the day's reading using her form as a guide. The group members will add to or correct her summary as necessary.

(4 Forms)

The Question Creator's job is to create and answer questions that go along with the day's reading. This role form often takes a little more time to "get the hang of." The Question Creator should pretend to be a teacher writing questions for students. There are four forms for this role. Some provide more guidance than others.

#1 of 4 (page 22) guides the Question Creator in writing questions. It uses the terms "lower-order" and "higher-order" to describe the two types of questions. Students will probably need coaching to understand the difference. Lower-order questions are questions that ask students about facts present within the text. For example, lower-order questions about *The Story of the Three Little Pigs* could include: "What materials did the three little pigs use to build their houses?" or "What kind of animal did the pigs fear?" Students who are having trouble reading or who have trouble with basic comprehension will benefit from going back to the text to find specific answers, because as they read to locate the specific facts, they remind themselves of other details in the text. Higher-order questions are questions with answers not readily available in the text. Students must think in order to compose these questions and look for the answers. Higher-order questions can measure reading comprehension, but they can also show how students are making other connections to the text. For example, questions such as, "How was the third little pig different from his brothers?" or "If you were planning to build a house, what materials would you use? Why?" make students think critically to find answers.

#2 of 4 (page 23) is less structured. It requires the Question Creator to make up and answer two questions, but suggests that the questions be "thinking questions." In order to support the student in writing these questions, the form suggests that the questions start with "Why" or "How." This often helps students get away from the predictable, closed questions that often start with "Who" or "What," and pushes them to write more open-ended, critical-thinking questions.

#3 of 4 (page 24) is fairly structured and provides the student with guidance and support. This form focuses on questions about the characters in the story. The first three questions are partially written, and the student needs only to fill in the blanks to finish the questions. This form, however, also provides the student with an opportunity to write his own question at the bottom of the page.

#4 of 4 (page 25) requires the Question Creator to create and answer six questions, but requires that each question begin with one of the "Five Ws" (and "One H"): Who, What, When, Where, Why, and How. This form allows the student to be creative and think of his own questions, while still providing support that is often needed by giving specific, higher-order prompts.

Regardless of the form used, when the Question Creator shares in his literature circle, he should read the question he created and allow his group members to use the book to answer it. After the group members have answered the question, the Question Creator should read his own answer in order to agree or disagree with the group members' answers. This is an area that often leads to healthy debates!

(3 Forms)

The Imaginative Illustrator's job is to visualize and illustrate a scene from the day's reading. This is an important, but often overlooked, reading strategy. Students respond well to being told that they have a "Brain TV" in their heads, and they should "see" everything that occurs in the reading. Using the term "TV" as opposed to "imagination" often helps them realize that, as they are reading, they should see action in their minds, much the way they would on a TV screen. Having them draw what they see in their heads helps them to internalize visualization as a natural reading strategy.

#1 of 3 (page 26) requires the Imaginative Illustrator to choose a scene, illustrate it, and explain why she chose this scene. This helps the student think about the scene selection, and hopefully guides her to choose a particularly detailed scene.

#2 of 3 (page 27) is probably the ideal form. It requires the student to indicate the words and phrases from the text that helped her visualize what she wants to draw for the scene. This helps the student recognize the author's craft, pick out details, and realize the importance of clear, descriptive, good writing. When explaining and modeling this role form it is important to stress that the reader should not simply copy a part of the scene, but should identify specific descriptive words and phrases, such as: "The water drop sparkled as it paused on the tip of his nose," or "The sheer, white clouds sailed across the icy blue sky."

#3 of 3 (page 28) is the simplest and is a good choice for struggling or younger readers. The student is required only to illustrate what she saw in her "Brain TV" while reading the day's selection. This allows the student to focus on reading comprehension and illustrating. It also gives the student more leeway in what she draws. This is a good form for a student who has trouble visualizing or describing what she sees as she reads.

When the Imaginative Illustrator shares in the literature circle, she should tell the group members to turn to the particular scene and follow along as she reads the scene aloud, then shares her illustration. The group members should then comment appropriately or ask questions.

(6 Forms)

The Word Watcher's job is to find and define vocabulary words from the day's reading. There are two main forms for this role, but there are three variations of each form. Therefore, there are six reproducibles altogether. Depending on the form, students will define the vocabulary words with either a dictionary or context clues, and will define either teacher-selected or student-selected words. The first three Word-Watcher forms require students to use a dictionary to define the words, while the last three forms require students to use context clues to write their own definitions for the vocabulary words. By glancing at the top, left corner of each reproducible, you can easily see whether the vocabulary words for each form are to be teacher-selected, student-selected, or both.

#1a of 6 (teacher-selected, page 29) requires the Word Watcher to find and define words that are teacher selected. Therefore, if the class uses one book, the Word Watchers work with the same words. This is extremely effective if you want students to identify specific words in the book, or if students are not yet prepared to select their own vocabulary words. Students use dictionaries to define these words.

#1b of 6 (teacher- and student-selected, page 30) is the same format as the previous role form, but it requires the Word Watcher to select two vocabulary words. This form lets you pick important words from the book while providing the student with an opportunity to look for and work with words he feels are important. When teaching the class how to complete this role form, model word selection so that students know how to choose vocabulary words. Explain that they may select words that they don't know, find interesting, catch their attention, think are important, etc.

#1c of 6 (student-selected, page 31) is the same format as #1a and #2a, but allows the student to choose his own words. This is a good choice for giving students more ownership of the activity, and it allows each group to work with a different set of words. Because the Word Watchers will probably select different words, it may be effective to discuss and list the vocabulary words selected during the closing whole-class discussion (see Chapter 2).

#2a of 6 (teacher-selected, page 32) is the same as #1a, except that the Word Watcher uses context clues instead of a dictionary to define the words. When teaching students how to complete this role form, model the use of context clues to figure out unknown words while reading. This lesson may take more time, and students may require ongoing practice to grasp this concept. It is a useful reading strategy, however, and one that students will benefit greatly from knowing.

#2b of 6 (teacher- and student-selected, page 33) and #2c of 6 (student-selected, page 34) follow the same formats as #1b and #1c, respectively. #2b and #2c require the Word Watcher to use context clues instead of a dictionary.

When the Word Watcher shares in his circle, he should first read the word, have the group members turn to the page in the book where it can be found, read the sentence or phrase containing the word, and then define the word. Group members' responses will vary depending on the form you select. For example, if the Word Watcher uses any #1 forms, and defines the vocabulary words using a dictionary, he can simply read the definition and the group members will discuss how that word's definition makes the meaning of the passage more clear. If, however, the Word Watcher uses any #2 forms and defines the words using context clues, then the group members should take turns saying what they think each word means, and what context clues they used from the book to come up with that definition. In addition, if the Word Watcher selected any or all of the vocabulary words, he should tell his group members why he selected those words.

Bridge Builder

(3 Forms)

The Bridge Builder's job is to make a connection, or "bridge," between the story and her own life. This role form is very open-ended because the responses will differ from student to student. The Bridge Builder can truly interact with the literature by bringing her own experiences and prior knowledge to the reading situation. There are three forms for this role.

#1 of 3 (page 35) provides the Bridge Builder with prompts in order to help her make connections. The student simply fills in the blanks. This role form provides direction and support for the student while still encouraging her to make personal connections between the book and her life.

#2 of 3 (page 36) is more open-ended and provides less support. The Bridge Builder writes about any connections she makes while reading, in any form she chooses: sentences, paragraphs, or notes. The directions on this form provide clues for the student by prompting her to think about herself, people she knows, movies she has seen, books she has read, etc.

#3 of 3 (page 37) also provides the student with support. It asks the Bridge Builder questions in order to guide her to make personal connections, but it is more open-ended than #1.

When the Bridge Builder shares in her circle, she should identify the excerpt from the day's reading she is talking about, read it aloud while the group members follow along, and then share her role form. The group members should then take turns sharing events they were reminded of from their own lives.

Circle Supervisor

(1 Form)

The entire process within each group is "supervised" by one student, the Circle Supervisor. In addition to completing an assigned role form and participating in the literature circle discussion, the Circle Supervisor ensures that the group is functioning efficiently and communicating in a positive manner. As students become more comfortable within their literature circles, the Circle Supervisor's job becomes almost nonexistent, because students want to participate and know what is expected. The Circle Supervisor only redirects fellow group members, if necessary, when you are not nearby. However, you may find that, with a good Circle Supervisor in place, your role in supervising the groups becomes less necessary, even for the group in which you are participating. The Circle Supervisor Form (page 38) should be introduced to all students before they begin meeting in their literature circle groups.

Assigning the Role Forms to Students

Although you will certainly want to assign role forms to students based on their needs and reading levels, how you assign the role forms to students is also a matter of personal preference. If all students are reading the same book and they have similar reading levels, it is much easier for each group to use the same forms for each role. This makes teaching the forms, reviewing the forms, comparing students' output, and keeping records much simpler. It also means that when the whole class meets and is reading the same book, all Story Summarizers, all Imaginative Illustrators, etc., can talk about and compare their responses, because they are all responding to the same prompt.

If, however, some students would do better with certain forms, or if you prefer to add variety so students are exposed to different strategies, then use the forms at your discretion. You can also start out using one form for each role and then switch to a different form for the next book. For example, everyone uses #1 of each role form for book one, but for book two you introduce and use #2 of each role form. There will be some overlap, since there are more versions of some forms, but everyone will get a chance to use each role form if this method is used.

Role forms should be assigned after you have determined the texts to be used and the group assignments. These processes are discussed thoroughly in Chapter 3, "Getting Literature Circles Going in the Classroom." Evaluating or assessing the role forms on a regular basis will demonstrate which students need more help with the process or the reading, and which students are ready to advance to more difficult role forms.

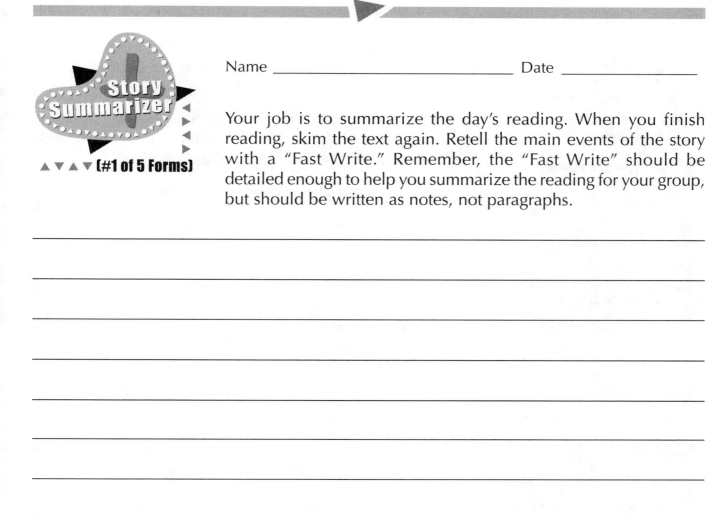

Story Summarizer

▲ ▼ ▲ ▼ **(#1 of 5 Forms)**

Name _____ Date _____

Your job is to summarize the day's reading. When you finish reading, skim the text again. Retell the main events of the story with a "Fast Write." Remember, the "Fast Write" should be detailed enough to help you summarize the reading for your group, but should be written as notes, not paragraphs.

_____

_____

_____

_____

_____

_____

_____

_____

_____

_____

_____

_____

_____

_____

_____

_____

_____

_____

Name _____ Date _____

Your job is to summarize the day's reading. When you finish reading, skim the text again. Write a summary of the reading using the "Somebody-Wanted-But-So Then" chart below.

SOMEBODY
(Character/s)

WANTED
(Goal)

BUT
(Problem)

SO THEN
(Solution)

Story Summarizer

(#3 of 5 Forms)

Name ______________________ Date ______________

Your job is to summarize the day's reading. When you finish reading, skim the text again. Write a summary of the reading in paragraph form. Remember to include only the most important parts of the day's reading.

Name _____ Date _____

Your job is to summarize the day's reading. When you finish reading, skim the text again. Then, fill in the story map below.

Character(s):

Setting:

Main events in order:

Problem(s) the main character is facing:

Possible solution(s):

Name _____ Date _____

Your job is to summarize the day's reading. Illustrate the day's reading and then retell it in your own words, using the blanks below. In the box, draw a picture to show what you read about.

Fill in the blanks to retell what you read about.

The first thing that happened is _____

_____

Then, _____

_____

The last thing that happened is _____

_____

Name _____ Date _____

Your job is to create and answer questions that go with the day's reading. Use what you have learned about "lower-order" and "higher-order" questions to make up and answer two questions. **At least one question must be higher-order.** Remember that higher-order questions really make you think. You must use your own knowledge, in addition to what the story said, to answer higher-order questions. Lower-order questions are easier to answer because you can find the answers in the story. Use a prompt below or make up your own questions.

Lower-Order Prompts

What . . . ?

When . . . ?

Who . . . ?

Where . . . ?

Higher-Order Prompts

Why do you think . . . ?

What would you do if . . . ?

What might have made the character . . . ?

How do you think . . . ?

How was . . . ?

If you . . . ?

Question 1: _____

_____

_____

Answer: _____

_____

_____

Question 2: _____

_____

_____

Answer: _____

_____

_____

Name _____ Date _____

Your job is to create and answer questions that go with the day's reading. Make up and answer two questions that ask your group members to tell something important about the reading. Your questions should start with "Why" or "How," and they should be questions that will make your group members think. Be creative and think about what was important in the reading.

Question 1: _____

_____

_____

_____

Answer: _____

_____

_____

_____

Question 2: _____

_____

_____

_____

Answer: _____

_____

_____

_____

Question Creator

▲▼▲▼ (#3 of 4 Forms)

Name ______________________________ Date ________________

Your job is to create and answer questions that go with the day's reading. Use the prompts below to help you get started. Use the last blank question line to make up your own question about the day's reading.

Question 1: Why do you think the character ______________________________

____

Answer: ____

____

____

Question 2: How do you think the character __________________ felt when ______________

____

Answer: ____

____

____

Question 3: If you were ______________________, what would you do if ____________________

____

Answer: ____

____

Question 4: ____

____

Answer: ____

____

 © Carson-Dellosa

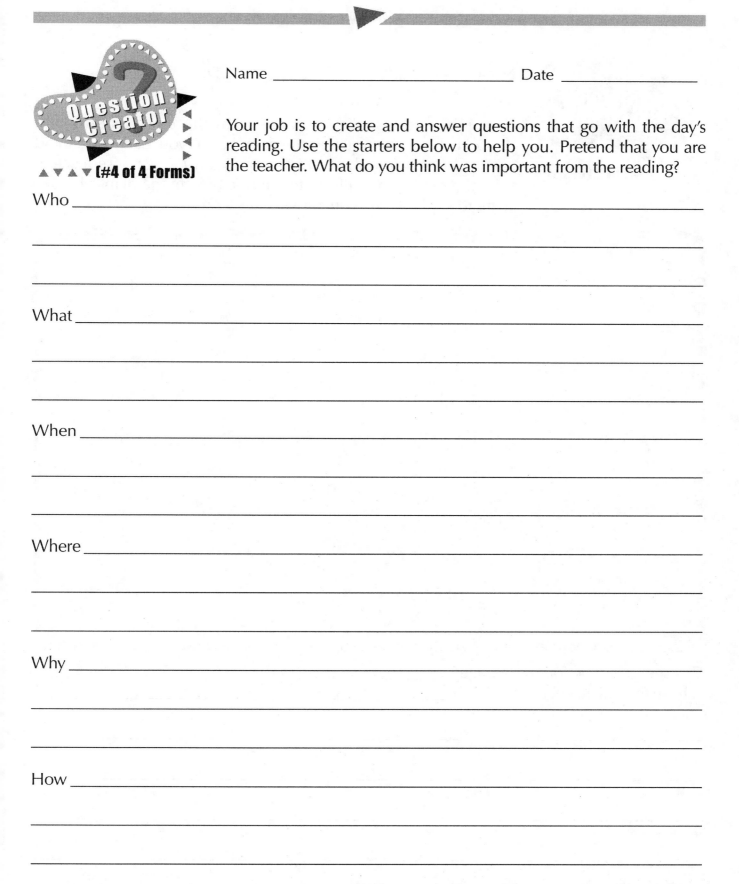

Question Creator

Name _____ Date _____

Your job is to create and answer questions that go with the day's reading. Use the starters below to help you. Pretend that you are the teacher. What do you think was important from the reading?

Who _____

_____

_____

What _____

_____

_____

When _____

_____

_____

Where _____

_____

_____

Why _____

_____

_____

How _____

_____

_____

Imaginative Illustrator

Name _____ Date _____

Your job is to visualize a scene from the day's reading and illustrate it for your group. Remember that, as you read, you should see the action from the text in your "Brain TV." Choose a scene from the reading and illustrate it in the box. In the blanks below, write to explain why you chose that scene.

This scene can be found on page _____
I chose this scene because _____

_____

_____

_____

_____

Name _____ Date _____

Your job is to visualize a scene from the day's reading and illustrate it for your group. Remember that, as you read, you should see the action from the text in your "Brain TV." Choose a scene from the reading and illustrate it in the box. Remember that you should choose a scene that has good details and descriptive words. Then, fill in the blanks below.

This scene can be found on page _____

Some of the words and phrases the author uses to help me visualize this scene in my head are:

_____

_____

_____

_____

Imaginative Illustrator (#3 of 3 Forms)

Name _____ Date _____

Your job is to illustrate what you see in your "Brain TV" while you are reading. Use the box below for your illustration. Remember to include details from the reading in your drawing.

This scene can be found on page _____ .

Word Watcher

Name _____ Date _____

Your job is to find and define vocabulary words from the day's reading. Write each word, the page number where you find the word, the sentence in which the word is used, and the dictionary definition of each word.

1. Word _____ Page #____ Sentence from reading _____

_____

Dictionary definition _____

_____

2. Word _____ Page #____ Sentence from reading _____

_____

Dictionary definition _____

_____

3. Word _____ Page #____ Sentence from reading _____

_____

Dictionary definition _____

_____

4. Word _____ Page #____ Sentence from reading _____

_____

Dictionary definition _____

_____

5. Word _____ Page #____ Sentence from reading _____

_____

Dictionary definition _____

_____

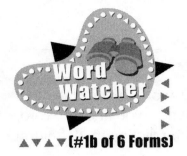

▲ ▼ ▲ ▼ (#1b of 6 Forms)

**teacher- and
*student-selected**

Name _____ Date _____

Your job is to find and define vocabulary words from the day's reading. Numbers 1, 2, and 3 are for the class vocabulary words. Numbers 4 and 5 are for you to choose from the day's reading. Write each word, the page number where the word is found, the sentence in which the word is used, and the dictionary definition.

1. Word _____ Page #____ Sentence from reading _____

_____

Dictionary definition _____

_____

2. Word _____ Page #____ Sentence from reading _____

_____

Dictionary definition _____

_____

3. Word _____ Page #____ Sentence from reading _____

_____

Dictionary definition _____

_____

*4. Word _____ Page #____ Sentence from reading _____

_____

Dictionary definition _____

_____

*5. Word _____ Page #____ Sentence from reading _____

_____

Dictionary definition _____

_____

_____

Word Watcher

▲ ▼ ▲ ▼ **[#1c of 6 Forms]**

student-selected

Name _____ Date _____

Your job is to find and define vocabulary words from the day's reading. As you read, choose words that you think are interesting, confusing, or new to you. Write each word, the page number where the word is found, the sentence in which the word is used, and the dictionary definition of the word. Be ready to tell your group why you chose these words.

1. Word _____ Page #____ Sentence from reading _____

   _____

   Dictionary definition _____

   _____

2. Word _____ Page #____ Sentence from reading _____

   _____

   Dictionary definition _____

   _____

3. Word _____ Page #____ Sentence from reading _____

   _____

   Dictionary definition _____

   _____

4. Word _____ Page #____ Sentence from reading _____

   _____

   Dictionary definition _____

   _____

5. Word _____ Page #____ Sentence from reading _____

   _____

   Dictionary definition _____

   _____

   _____

Word Watcher

teacher-selected

Name _____ Date _____

Your job is to find and define vocabulary words from the day's reading. Write each word, the page number where the word is found, the sentence in which the word is used, and the word's meaning. Use **context clues** (clues that you find in the reading) to figure out what each word means.

1. Word _____ Page #____ Sentence from reading _____

_____

Dictionary definition _____

_____

2. Word _____ Page #____ Sentence from reading _____

_____

Dictionary definition _____

_____

3. Word _____ Page #____ Sentence from reading _____

_____

Dictionary definition _____

_____

4. Word _____ Page #____ Sentence from reading _____

_____

Dictionary definition _____

_____

5. Word _____ Page #____ Sentence from reading _____

_____

Dictionary definition _____

_____

_____

Word Watcher

▲▼▲▼ **(#2b of 6 Forms)**

**teacher- and
*student-selected**

Name _____ Date _____

Your job is to find and define vocabulary words from the day's reading. Numbers 1, 2, and 3 are for the class vocabulary words. Numbers 4 and 5 are for you to choose from the day's reading. Write each word, the page number where the word is found, the sentence in which the word is used, and the word's meaning. Use **context clues** (clues that you find in the reading) to figure out what each word means.

1. Word _____ Page #_____ Sentence from reading _____

_____

Dictionary definition _____

_____

2. Word _____ Page #_____ Sentence from reading _____

_____

Dictionary definition _____

_____

3. Word _____ Page #_____ Sentence from reading _____

_____

Dictionary definition _____

_____

*4. Word _____ Page #_____ Sentence from reading _____

_____

Dictionary definition _____

_____

*5. Word _____ Page #_____ Sentence from reading _____

_____

Dictionary definition _____

_____

_____

Word Watcher

▲▼▲▼ **(#2c of 6 Forms)**

student-selected

Name _____ Date _____

Your job is to find and define vocabulary words from the day's reading. As you read, choose words that you think are interesting, confusing, or new to you. Write each word, the page number where the word is found, the sentence in which the word is used, and the word's meaning. Use **context clues** (clues that you find in the reading) to figure out what each word means. Be ready to tell your group why you chose these words.

1. Word _____ Page #_____ Sentence from reading _____

_____

Dictionary definition _____

_____

2. Word _____ Page #_____ Sentence from reading _____

_____

Dictionary definition _____

_____

3. Word _____ Page #_____ Sentence from reading _____

_____

Dictionary definition _____

_____

4. Word _____ Page #_____ Sentence from reading _____

_____

Dictionary definition _____

_____

5. Word _____ Page #_____ Sentence from reading _____

_____

Dictionary definition _____

_____

_____

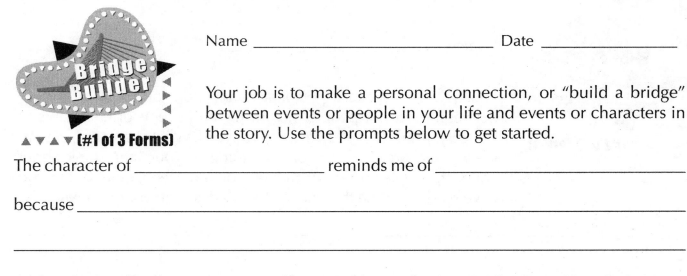

Name _____ Date _____

Your job is to make a personal connection, or "build a bridge" between events or people in your life and events or characters in the story. Use the prompts below to get started.

The character of _____ reminds me of _____

because _____

_____

_____

_____

I know how the character _____ felt when _____

_____

because _____

_____

_____

_____

The part on page _____, when _____

_____

reminds me of _____

_____

_____

_____

_____

Name _____ Date _____

Your job is to make a personal connection, or "build a bridge" between events or people in your life and events or characters in the story. Think of your own life as you read. What characters, events, scenes, etc., remind you of something in your life? Think about yourself, people you know, movies you have seen, other books you have read, etc. Use the lines below to describe your connections.

_____

_____

_____

_____

_____

_____

_____

_____

_____

_____

_____

_____

_____

_____

_____

_____

Bridge Builder

▲ ▼ ▲ ▼ (#3 of 3 Forms)

Name _____ Date _____

Your job is to make a personal connection, or "build a bridge" between events or people in your life and events or characters in the story. Use the questions below to get started.

1. Do any of the characters in this book remind you of any characters from other books you have read? If so, who and why? _____

_____

_____

_____

2. Do any of the characters in this book remind you of anyone you know? If so, who and why?

_____

_____

_____

_____

3. Pick an event from the reading that reminds you of something that happened to you or someone you know. What scene is it and what does it remind you of?

_____

_____

_____

4. What would you do if you were _____, a character from this book?

_____

_____

_____

Circle Supervisor

▲ ▽ ▲ ▽ ▲ ▽ ▲ **(1 Form)**

Name _____ Date _____

Your job is to guide the group throughout the literature circle discussion. Remember that you are like the teacher when the teacher is not around.

Take turns and follow this order so that all of the group members have a chance to share their roles.

1. Story Summarizer
2. Question Creator
3. Imaginative Illustrator
4. Word Watcher
5. Bridge Builder

Tips and Reminders

▶ Stay on task. If your group starts talking about something other than the literature, then it's your job to politely get them back on track.

▶ Remember that all circle members should have a chance to share their roles and discuss the reading.

▶ Use positive language at all times. Here are some phrases you can use to encourage your circle members:

- "Nice job!"
- "I hadn't thought of it that way!"
- "Great try. I was thinking . . ."
- "Let's get back on track, everyone."
- "Maybe you're right. I thought . . ."

Getting Literature Circles Going in the Classroom

Literature circles can be complicated and a little intimidating. Implementing them requires planning, modeling, and organizing. This chapter will help you get literature circles going in a step-by-step, manageable, and realistic way. All aspects of start-up are covered, including classroom management and implementation of each step. Getting started does require some effort, but once the program is underway, the students are in charge, and you will truly adapt to the role of facilitator. You will quickly realize how easy and worthwhile the process is.

This Chapter Includes:

Step-by-step instructions for integrating literature circles.

* introducing the concept to students

* selecting and obtaining books

* selecting and rotating groups

* teaching students how to "do" literature circles

* defining the teacher's role

* getting through the first day

* assessing the work

Introducing the Concept to Students

Objectives:

• Make sure students know the steps of literature circles.

• Help students develop enthusiasm and a comfort level for a new way to study literature.

The first step is to talk to students about how literature circles work. Do this by briefly explaining the roles and worksheets, the schedule (even if you don't know exactly, you can estimate how long it may take), the assessment (see pages 56-59), and most importantly, the books and book selection process. Once students get an idea of what they will be doing, they become excited, motivated, and ready to learn.

Selecting and Obtaining Books

Objectives:
- determining who will select books
- choosing the literature
- acquiring book sets

Determining Who Will Select Books
After introducing the concept of literature circles, the next step in the process is to decide whether you assign the literature or if students will choose literature themselves. When literature circles are new to students (and to you as well!), it is a good idea for you to select the literature. This will eliminate the logistical problems that can arise when students are doing the selecting, and will help you take advantage of books that are easy to provide.

As students become more familiar with the process, consider helping them work toward choosing their own books for the literature circle activities. This gives students more ownership and invests them more in the activity because they have a stake in making the books "work." They want to read the books they have chosen; it becomes more than just an assignment. However, that is not always feasible or practical. You know your students best, and you know whether they are ready for such a challenge. Perhaps they are not ready yet, but soon will be, or perhaps they could select books with guidance. Or, perhaps they are ready to select their own books, but *you* are not! It's your decision. Refer to the Book Selection worksheet on page 60 to help students choose books.

If you let students select their own books, it is your job to give them choices. Provide a number of related or themed "text sets" and allow students to choose the book or books they want to read. For example, you may ask students to select from a pet-themed text set consisting of *Old Yeller* by Fred Gipson (HarperCollins, 1956), *Shiloh* by Phyllis Reynolds Naylor (Atheneum, 1991), *Because of Winn-Dixie* by Kate DiCamillo (Candlewick Press, 2000), and *Where the Red Fern Grows* by Wilson Rawls (Doubleday, 1961). Refer to the book list (pages 61-63) for more ideas.

Choosing the Literature
Much of the criteria you will use to select books will depend on the curriculum in your school, as well as on students' needs and abilities. Following are general guidelines to keep in mind when choosing books for literature circle groups.

First and foremost, the books should be "quality authentic literature." Literature circle groups are not the venue for responding to basal-type reading materials such as "consumables," worksheets, activity kits, etc.

Obviously, the literature must be appropriate for the general reading level of the class as a whole. Chapter 4 demonstrates how literature circles help both struggling readers and more proficient readers. Therefore, it is fine to select literature that is generally appropriate for your grade level.

If you want to start with the same book for the whole class, then obtain a class set of the book. You may be thinking, "Enough copies of one book for my whole class?" Don't panic! See page 42, which lists ways to obtain books.

If you choose not to use the same book for the whole class (whether due to your preference or book supply limitations), each literature circle group can use a different book, which means you will only have to come up with a handful of each title. Using more than one title simultaneously is a very effective way to do literature circles because the groups can take turns reading different books, and can compare or contrast among the books during whole-class discussions.

If literature circle groups are starting off with different books, think about using the same author, theme, or genre, so that there is some type of uniformity among the books being read. Having a theme allows for more opportunities to create non-literature-circles activities that can supplement your reading. For example, if you use the pet theme suggested on page 40, consider creating a supplemental unit around pets in another curriculum area (such as science or art) to go along with your theme.

Basing the theme on one author will give students a chance to study the author's biography, country of origin, or historical context. For example, if literature circle groups read different books by Laura Ingalls Wilder, they will also learn from participating in activities about the pioneers, Native American traditions, and US history from that time period. You may also decide to have groups read different books from one series. This works well for several reasons. First, whole-class discussion is fun with books in a series because the characters will be familiar. Second, the books are on similar levels for all groups. Finally, interesting discussions come from comparing how the same characters behave in different situations.

Building a theme around a particular genre may limit you to literary and writing activities, but you can still create effective projects for students. For example, assigning age-appropriate poetry by Robert Frost, e. e. cummings, Lewis Carroll, and others will expose students to many poets (especially in the whole-class discussion), and will inspire them to write their own poems. You can also choose a set of nature poems, poems specifically for children, fantasy poems, etc., to create your theme.

For more help with creating themes, use the Book and Theme Suggestions list on pages 61-63. This list consists of popular children's books, and suggests ways to group them according to theme. Also, experiment with letting students create their own book lists with themes. List several possible themes and have students suggest books they feel are appropriate for each.

To introduce students to and inform them about their choices, give a "book talk" (a brief description and review of each book). Then, allow students to choose the books they want to read. Use the Book Selection worksheet on page 60 to help students make their preferences known to you. Keep in mind that you may have to help students choose books (or even assign books) based on their skill levels. You should genuinely be excited about the book(s) you choose for the literature circles. This is especially critical when you, and not the students, select the books.

Acquiring Book Sets

How many copies of each book you need will be determined by whether students use the same book or several different books at the same time. If you want all students to read the same book, plan on acquiring one book for each child. However, if you decide to use text sets, and each group reads a different book with a common theme, then you will only need a book for every group member. It is obviously much easier to get a few copies of the same book than it is to get a classroom set.

Regardless of how many copies you need, there are many ways to increase the size of your classroom library. Use the Donation Letter (page 54) to request donations from parents, local businesses, bookstores, etc., or check into one or more of the resources below.

Scout your school. Your school library may have multiple copies that you are not aware of. Use your colleagues—you can usually find at least one teacher in your school who is a "book collector" and would loan you books.

Search local bookstores—especially larger franchises—because they usually offer discounts to teachers. Some even provide teachers with membership cards that offer a consistent discount from each purchase price.

Remember to shop at used bookstores—they can be gold mines for educators!

Don't overlook garage sales and flea markets. Children's books at garage sales can be priced as low as ten cents or less!

Join a school book club. They are excellent sources for purchasing books at discount prices, and they often offer free books as incentives for teachers.

Apply for grants. Although harder to come by, a grant is an excellent way to acquire funds for books.

Finally, ask parents to help. The feasibility of this option will depend on your school population. Once parents understand why their children need these books, if they are able, they are often happy to cooperate. Simply use the Donation Letter (page 54) or a Parents' Night to explain your reading program and the benefits of using authentic literature. Provide parents with a book wish list, or incorporate your request into a school fund-raiser.

Selecting and Rotating Groups

Objectives:

- deciding what factors will determine group selection
- planning a system for group rotation

Deciding What Factors Will Determine Group Selection

Each "circle" is considered a group. There are many ways to select group members. The important thing to remember is that each circle must be small and efficient. Groups of four to six students are usually best.

If students select books and then form groups accordingly, group size will be determined by the number of students interested in a particular title. If you choose this method of group selection but anticipate having more requests for a book than you have copies available, have students list a few books in order of their preferences so that you can try to give everyone their first or second choice. If you use several books at once, use the Book Selection worksheet (page 60) to help students choose their books.

If the groups are not based on literature selection, there are several decisions to make about how to form groups. Sometimes teachers need to step in and choose who will work with whom. There is the question of using heterogeneous groups (students with mixed abilities) versus homogeneous groups (students with similar abilities). Heterogeneous grouping can be very effective in literature circles, because more proficient readers support struggling ones. However, homogeneous grouping may better meet the needs of some students.

As you select groups, remember that every class is different—there are some years when students just seem to work well together, and there are years when, regardless of great effort on your part, student-selected groups lead to conflict. Sometimes, you have to use trial and error; experiment with one type of selection method and adjust as necessary.

Especially after students have been participating in literature circles effectively for some time, they will probably be ready to choose their own groups because they will know what is expected of them. Allowing students to form their own groups, as long as they show they can do it in an effective manner, can serve as a reward for successful group work.

Planning a System for Group Rotation

As long as the groups are working well together, most teachers who use literature circles recommend having the groups remain the same throughout the course of a book. Working with the same group members helps students develop a rapport with each other, meaning that these students will get used to working together throughout the duration of a book, and will often develop their own dialogue. Additionally, group members can refer back to a discussion that may have occurred during a previous meeting, or make connections between one chapter and another.

But, after the first book is completed, don't let things get too comfortable. Create new groups each time you start a new book, so that students work with new classmates each time. Introducing new combinations of students keeps the process fresh and interesting. If there is tension between group members, it will give you the opportunity to change the situation. Also, you will be able to assign readers to groups with students who have complementary skills. For example, you can pair a strong reader with a weaker one, or a student who is good at asking questions and soliciting answers with a student who is reluctant to speak.

Teaching Students How to "Do" Literature Circles

Objectives:

- explaining and modeling role forms
- allotting time for group meetings
- choosing group meeting spaces
- informing groups about where to meet
- organizing supplies, groups, and roles
- modeling literature circle action

Explaining and Modeling Role Forms

After having the general classroom discussion about literature circles, it's time to start training students how to do each step. Just like the training in this book, student training should begin with role forms. The reproducible role forms in Chapter 2 cover key story elements such as comprehension, vocabulary, visualization, summarizing, etc. Each role has several different forms, which are formatted differently. Select the form you prefer for each role. (For example: there are five different forms for the role of Story Summarizer, so choose the form you prefer to use with your students. Of course, you can always have students in different groups use different forms, or modify the role forms to suit individual students by making them easier or more difficult.)

Modeling and teaching one role at a time, especially at the beginning, helps clarify the requirements for each role. Begin by reading a selection from something with which the students are familiar. Place a transparency of the role form (such as the Story Summarizer form) on an overhead projector to let students see you complete the page as they would. (Some teachers prefer to model this role form on the board or even in small groups, depending on what they feel is the best format for their students.) Explain and model the completion of the form by thinking aloud and explaining each step as you complete it. After the exercise, have students read another selection and complete Story-Summarizer role forms on their own. Review their work and make adjustments or reteach if necessary.

Once students truly understand how to do this first role form, repeat the process until they know how to complete all of the role forms they will need for their literature circles. If you choose to teach one a day, students will be ready to start literature circles after only a few days. The total number of role forms you choose to teach (and then use) for each role may depend on how quickly students

pick up on the process. For example, if you have four students in each literature circle, you will select four different role forms, such as #1 of Story Summarizer, Word Watcher, Imaginative Illustrator, and Question Creator, that the class will have to learn how to do. Students usually respond best to learning one role at a time, especially at the beginning. Once students know how to do literature circles, it will be simple to add role forms to or substitute for those that students have already used.

Allotting Time for Group Meetings

As you set up the time expectations for literature circles, it is crucial to do what works best for students and for the class routine. There is no set time frame, but usually the whole process takes about 60 minutes. The average breakdown is as follows:

- 35 minutes for independent reading and role form completion
- 20 minutes for circle discussions
- 10 minutes for whole-class discussion

The amount of time allotted for each part of the literature circles process is another aspect of literature circles that is dictated by the teacher's needs and preferences. If only a limited amount of time is available for literature circles, shorten the allotted class time for the reading assignment and ask students to read more for homework. Another option is to have students complete the reading as a homework assignment, so they will be ready to complete the role forms and meet during class time. Or, have students read and complete the role forms during one class session, and meet to discuss on the following day. Make sure that role forms are completed during class time on occasion, and periodically check that students who did them for homework actually complete them, since group discussion is dependent upon preparation.

On the other hand, students may be so involved within their circles that you decide to extend the time allotted so that they can continue their discussions. It is important to note, however, that the independent reading should not be too lengthy. If you make the reading assignment too long, some students may be overwhelmed, and their comprehension and responses will suffer. Focus on quality, not quantity.

Choosing Group Meeting Spaces

The size and layout of your classroom will largely determine your students' group meeting locations. If you have a large, open classroom, then simply assign locations around the room so that groups will not interfere with each other. If there is limited space, you will have to be more creative. It's surprising how well children can focus in small groups, even when surrounded by other groups.

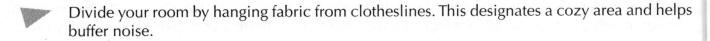

Use as much of the classroom space as possible, but if necessary, have students meet at their desks or on the floor. Or, try one of these options.

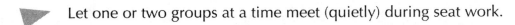

Divide your room by hanging fabric from clotheslines. This designates a cozy area and helps buffer noise.

Let one or two groups at a time meet (quietly) during seat work.

Use blankets on the floor to designate meeting spaces (the idea is for students to stay on their own group's blanket).

Push desks into completely new arrangements just for literature circles to create a break between this and other schoolwork.

If a teacher in a nearby classroom has a different lunch schedule, ask to use that space and schedule your literature circle time accordingly.

Another thing to consider when assigning group meeting spaces is the noise level. With a classroom full of students talking and even sometimes debating in groups, it will not be quiet, especially if they become passionate about the books they are reading. The noise level can take getting used to. It can also pose a problem for surrounding classrooms or for a teacher whose room is in a studio setting. If there are other classes nearby, train students to whisper or talk softly while in their groups. Use a bell or other signal to let them know when the volume is getting too high. Praise and reward groups who are working quietly and efficiently.

An ideal solution for a small or overly noisy classroom is to go outside of it. Prop open the classroom door and have one or two groups meet in the hallway away from other rooms. Reserve a section of the library for "remote" meetings. If your room opens to a field or outdoor area, have another group take advantage of that space. Before students leave the classroom, make sure they know the rules for being outside the room. Depending on the students' ages and how well they are able to monitor themselves, you may choose to allow them increased meeting freedom as a reward for holding quiet, responsible group meetings.

Informing Groups about Where to Meet

To avoid confusion or conflict, mark the group areas with colorful tape, affix small signs to the floor or walls, or display a small classroom map with the group locations. You may also post copies of the different book covers, or let students design signs which depict themes, characters, or events in their books.

Organizing Supplies, Groups, and Role Forms

In order for literature circles to run efficiently, students must know at a glance where their supplies are kept, what groups they are in, and which roles they are playing. Especially if the whole class is reading the same book, students may have trouble keeping even their groups in mind at first, not to mention which role forms they need each day. Fortunately, there are not many supplies to organize for literature circles: just the book sets, role forms, and any materials students need to understand what their roles are and where their groups meet.

One easy option for supply storage is to have students keep track of the role forms and/or the text sets. Students can have their own role form folders in which they keep blank copies of all of the role forms they will be doing. They can also keep any completed role forms that you do not collect in these folders. With a folder system, once students get comfortable with literature circles, you will just have to remind them of their roles for the day and assign the reading selection. They will then take out the required forms and get to work. The folders are also practical because students have all of their literature circle forms together, making it easy for students to refer back to them to see their growth and improvement. Students may also like to keep books at their desks. If a student reads ahead, it is easier for her to keep a bookmark in the book.

Another easy option is to create a literature circle center in which books and blank role forms are stored. Each student will be able to go to the center, choose a book, find her assigned role form, and start on the day's reading, all at her own pace. This will eliminate stray papers and extra role forms being wasted, since students won't have a chance to misplace them, but it may mean that books are handled more often and therefore will not last as long.

Once you decide how to organize supplies, focus on organizing students—a bigger challenge! One simple and effective way to organize students' roles is to have a literature circle chart in your room. You can make it on a bulletin board, a laminated piece of poster board, or a pocket chart. Write the students' names on index cards and copy the role tags from page 55. Organize each group horizontally on one line. You can either rotate the students' name cards from pocket to pocket each time you do literature circles or rotate the role cards. Rotate cards before each literature circle session so students are aware of their roles.

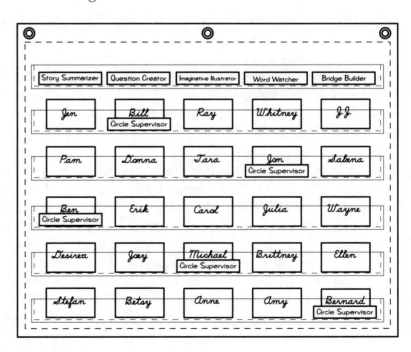

Another way to help students remember their groups is to create role tags for them to wear. Laminate copies of the role tags from page 55 for each group, then punch holes in the tops and cut apart

the tags. Thread lengths of yarn to create role necklaces. You may want to choose a different color of yarn or different color of paper for each group, to help avoid confusion. To change roles, simply have students exchange necklaces. This method takes more time in the beginning because you have to make the necklaces, but it is more concrete for younger students.

To give students more ownership of the process, you may want to let them make and decorate their own class set of role tags (either using the reproducibles or index cards); then designate a special hook in the classroom on which to store them. Letting students decorate them in a theme similar to the book(s) they are reading will help students identify their tags and groups more easily.

Keeping track of the Circle Supervisor is similar to keeping track of other roles. Some teachers like to make the students who have particular roles always serve as the Circle Supervisors. For example, you may decide that the students who are serving as Imaginative Illustrators will always be the Circle Supervisors as well. Another way to indicate the Circle Supervisors for the day is to make colorful cards, then rotate those cards from pocket to pocket of the pocket chart (see page 47).

Regardless of how you choose to organize the groups, it is critical that you rotate the roles regularly, so that each student gets an opportunity to serve as a Circle Supervisor and practice the reading strategies on all of the different role forms you select. Rotating the roles also helps keep the process fresh and interesting for students.

Modeling Literature Circle Action for Students

After all of the preparation is finished and the classroom management decisions are made, it's time to teach students what to do in their circles. Be warned: no matter how many times or ways you go over the process, students will need some redirection. You can be clear with all of your directions, explanations, and expectations, but you will encounter problems the first couple of times you do literature circles. After several reteaching sessions, you and the students will adapt, and literature circles will run smoothly.

From watching you model the role forms, students know that after they read the day's literature they should complete their role forms independently. The next step is teaching them what you expect when they are in their groups. Remember that literature circles are groups of students who are reading the same book and gathering to discuss their reading. You want students to read, complete the role form, and then gather in their groups to talk, share, and debate. The role forms are guides for the discussions and will serve as catalysts for debates. Explain that when groups meet, students should take turns sharing their role form responses and exploring each other's thoughts.

For example, a student named Pablo is a Story Summarizer for the day, so he will first share his role form responses and then turn to his group members and ask them each, in turn, what they would add. After all group members have shared, it is the next group member's turn.

Josephine is the Word Watcher, and it is now her turn to share her role form responses. She instructs her group members to look up the first word and asks one person to read the sentence. After she defines the new word using context clues, she asks her group members to comment on the meaning of the word while referring to the literature.

This process continues until all of the group members have shared their roles and discussed them with the other group members. Remember, the entire process is "supervised" by the Circle Supervisor, but as students get more comfortable, the Circle Supervisor's job becomes almost nonexistent, because the students want to participate and know what is expected. The Circle Supervisor only redirects fellow group members, if necessary, when you are not nearby.

The best way for students to understand what is expected is to explain briefly and then role-play. Select a group of students to demonstrate with you what a literature circle looks and sounds like. As the rest of the class looks on, participate in a literature circle and redirect students in your "group" if necessary. Depending on how much time you have allotted for this instruction and role-playing session, you may then choose to proceed with the actual first literature circle meetings or wait until the following day.

Defining the Teacher's Role

Objectives:
- deciding where to be during group work
- monitoring the "non-teacher" groups

Deciding Where to Be During Group Work
As teachers, we often hear buzz words such as "facilitator" and "guide." Unfortunately, curriculum needs and student needs don't always allow teachers to fill these roles. Literature circles provide the ideal environment for the teacher to serve as facilitator and guide. Exactly what you do during each session will depend on how long the class has been doing literature circles. If students are just learning the process, then you will be observing, redirecting, and role modeling. If they have been doing literature circles for a while and the program is well underway, you will still observe and occasionally redirect, but you will mainly participate.

Ideally, when students begin their independent reading for the day, you too will read independently. In this manner, you are serving as a role model as well as participating in the day's activities. As the students work on role forms independently, you can circulate around the room, assisting, if necessary, and encouraging on-task behavior. When some students finish their role forms early, remind them to go to their meeting spots and wait for the rest of their group members. Observe the "early birds" to ensure that they are not just sitting and waiting, but are rereading the selection, reviewing their work, completing Early Bird worksheets, (pages 73-76) etc.

After students have joined their groups, participate in the circle discussions. You can do this a number of ways. You may choose to sit in and participate with one group during the whole session and then switch groups next time. Keep in mind, however, that in order for this to be effective, your other groups must run smoothly and efficiently, because you will not be circulating. You may opt to record an audiotape of one or more groups when you are not available to work with everyone, particularly if you prefer to participate in one group per session.

Another, and often more practical option is to spend some time with each group. This way, you can observe, assess, and participate with several groups. How much time you spend with each group may depend on how involved you get in a particular circle, how much redirection that group needs, and/or how much time is allotted for literature circles on that day.

Once students get used to the idea that you will occasionally join a group, they will not be intimidated. Most of the time, elementary students actually want their teachers to join them, and will be especially eager and motivated. However, when first entering a group, it is a good idea just to sit and observe so the students realize that they should be doing the work. Also, if the discussion comes to a halt, you may want to prompt the students in order to encourage the continuation of the discussion.

Monitoring "Non-Teacher" Groups

The nature of literature circles in a well-run classroom is intrinsically motivating. Therefore, the students *should* participate, discuss, and "do what they're supposed to do" without much redirection, although, at first, it may not always work the way it should. The Circle Supervisors will be the ones to remind members to get "back on task" if necessary. Remember that they serve as the groups' teachers when you are not around. Students should recall how to act as Circle Supervisors from the teaching sessions, so they will know how to use positive language to keep the groups focused. If there are problems, use the management techniques mentioned previously, or refer to Chapter 4 for more information. Circulating around the room will diminish the possibility of off-task behaviors.

Another way to inspire groups to do well even when you are not present is to have students occasionally fill out assessment worksheets (page 56-59). There are four types of these worksheets. The Self-Assessment worksheet should be filled out by each student independently, giving him a chance to evaluate his performance and effort during each aspect of literature circle sessions. The Group Assessment worksheet can be filled out as a group, but you are more likely to get honest responses about the functionality of each group if students complete these independently as well. The Self/Group Assessment worksheet is a combination of these two that helps students evaluate their performances and efforts in terms of how well the rest of the group is working. It can help a weak participant take more responsibility for her own participation, and it can also motivate a strong participant to help her fellow group members more.

Finally, perhaps the best motivator is the Circle Star worksheet. Each student in the group should independently fill out a Circle Star worksheet, nominating one person as the "star" of the group. There are several ways to use this form. One way is as a progress report. Hopefully each student will be the "Circle Star" at some point, but if not, you can plan to observe those students and their group members more carefully. A second way is to help you decide, as you near the end of a book, how to create new groups for the next round of literature circles. You can evenly disperse your "Circle Stars" after you let students identify them for you. A third way is to motivate students during the process. Assign each group member a different person to write about on the Circle Star worksheet, so that each student reads positive feedback about herself. If you use the Circle Star worksheet in this way, model for the class how to find and write positive feedback.

Getting through the First Day

Objectives:

- classroom scenario

- bringing the class back together

- time to celebrate

It's time to try literature circles! The books have been selected, the groups formed, the roles assigned, and students know what to do! Following is an example of what the whole scenario might (hopefully!) sound like.

Classroom Scenario

Mrs. Aguerre: "All right, class, we are ready to have our first literature circles meeting. We will be reading chapter six of our class book. Let's refer to the Literature-Circle Pocket Chart to review who will be doing what job today. The Story Summarizers today are Pablo, Josephine, Beth, and Eric. Who can remind us what the Story Summarizers do?" (Students give answers until teacher is satisfied that they understand.) "The Word Watchers today are . . . ." (This repeats until all roles are reviewed. As students become more familiar with your literature circles management style, you can eliminate this step.)

"And finally, the Circle Supervisors today are Eric, Roxanne, Alicia, and Steven. Remember that the Circle Supervisors have their own role forms to complete and share, but also serve as the leaders of the group. Circle Supervisors are like the teachers when I am not around. They will remind their group members whose turn it is, remind them to use positive language like 'Good idea, but what else can we add to that answer?' and keep everyone on task. Now, does everyone remember where your group will be meeting when you're done with your reading and role forms? Good, any questions?"

After the teacher answers any questions, students begin their independent reading for the day. Once they finish, they work on their role forms at their desks. As students complete the role forms, they go to their predetermined meeting spots to wait for the rest of the group members to finish. During group work, the teacher circulates around the room, redirecting as necessary (remember that it will probably be necessary this early on!), joins groups for short periods, and observes. The teacher might hear the students interacting in the following manner.

Roxanne: "OK, Abby, you're the Word Watcher, right? What words did you write down from the chapter?"

Abby: "The first one I found was boisterous. It's on page 29, second paragraph." (Group members all turn to that page in their books and follow along as Abby reads the sentence in which the word is found.) "I think the word means crazy and loud because in that paragraph they're talking about how boisterous the party was with all of the kids running around. What do you think?"

This continues as all of the group members share their role-form responses and then ask the other group members to agree, disagree, add information, etc. The teacher continues to circulate and participate in groups until the time is up or most groups are finished.

Bringing the Class Back Together
The last part of literature circles, the whole-class discussion, can have several objectives. It can:

- serve as a review of the day's reading
- give closure to the lesson
- clear up any confusion or answer any questions that arise during the circles
- address any logistical problems (noise level, too much movement around the classroom, etc.)
- allow groups time to share how their meetings went and talk about what part of the reading they focused on
- provide students with feedback and praise so they can be more on track next time
- pass out any group- or self-assessment worksheets (see pages 56-59)

Use the wrap-up time for any purpose that is appropriate for your class. Teacher questions should be very open and broad when the class comes back together. Each wrap-up may be different because of students' needs, and it is a good idea to let them set the agenda and see where it goes. Here is an example of what bringing the groups back together may sound like.

Mrs. Aguerre: "Who would like to share what happened or what was discussed in the circles today?"

Ben: "In our group, we couldn't agree on whether Judy Moody's new recycling habits were really a good idea." (*Judy Moody Saves the World!* by Megan McDonald: Candlewick Press, 2002)

Mrs. Aguerre: "What do you mean? What was the debate?"

Xiomara: "Well, I thought that Judy was being obnoxious to her family. She just decided to start rearranging everything in the house, without even asking her parents! But, Ben and Sofia thought that Judy was doing something great for the earth, and it didn't matter how she did it."

Let students' interests help direct the conversation. This is the time for them to share with you what they learned and did well. Be sure to praise them when possible. At this point, you may also want to jot down notes about how the sessions seemed to go. If any of the groups seems not to have much to say, or limits their comments to negative or nonspecific remarks, plan to sit in with that group during the next literature circle session.

Time to Celebrate!

You did it! Your students have participated in their first literature circles. And, it should get better each time. Reward the class for doing a good job or consider a themed celebration when the first books are finished.

Assessing the Work

There are four assessment worksheets to choose from on pages 56-59.

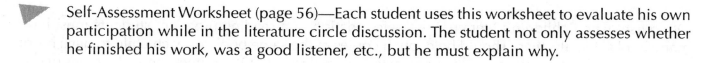 Self-Assessment Worksheet (page 56)—Each student uses this worksheet to evaluate his own participation while in the literature circle discussion. The student not only assesses whether he finished his work, was a good listener, etc., but he must explain why.

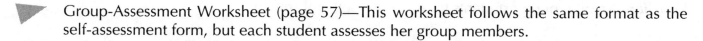 Group-Assessment Worksheet (page 57)—This worksheet follows the same format as the self-assessment form, but each student assesses her group members.

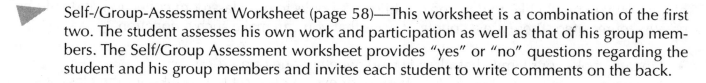 Self-/Group-Assessment Worksheet (page 58)—This worksheet is a combination of the first two. The student assesses his own work and participation as well as that of his group members. The Self/Group Assessment worksheet provides "yes" or "no" questions regarding the student and his group members and invites each student to write comments on the back.

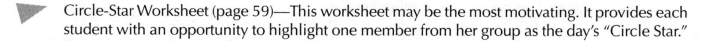 Circle-Star Worksheet (page 59)—This worksheet may be the most motivating. It provides each student with an opportunity to highlight one member from her group as the day's "Circle Star."

Using the Assessment Worksheets

You can use the assessment worksheets to evaluate students' performances during literature circles, but the assessment worksheets can also help you manage the groups. These assessment worksheets also provide students with a safe method to voice any concerns, confusions, or complaints that they may be too intimidated to mention verbally. When reading and comparing students' completed assessment forms, you may see patterns that alert you to potential or existing problems. For example, you may notice that a particular group's members are complaining about one member's lack of effort. Or, you may notice that one student's self-assessment indicates that he does not feel he is doing well in literature circles. Perhaps there is one student who is chosen as the "Circle Star" repeatedly, which could mean she is doing much more of the work than the rest of her group members.

You can pick and choose from the four assessment worksheets, depending on students' needs. You may want to use a different one each time, so that sometimes students are evaluating only themselves, the group members, or both. Some students do not handle group evaluations well (are not honest, use them to praise only their friends, etc.) and may benefit most from the self-assessment worksheets. The Circle Star worksheet may be used for every literature circle discussion, or perhaps sporadically, so that it is really a "big deal." One way to truly motivate students to do well enough to be nominated as a Circle Star is to make a bulletin board on which the Circle Stars are displayed each time. You may also want to send each student's Circle Star worksheets home to parents at the end of a literature circles unit.

Dear _____,

Research shows that quality literature should be the core of any good reading program. Therefore, we will be using children's books as part of our classroom reading curriculum. One of our most exciting literature-based activities will be literature circles. Literature circles are "circles" (groups) of approximately five students that gather on a regular basis to discuss the book(s) they are reading in class. The purpose of literature circles is to get students to think about, discuss, and even debate quality literature.

Of course, when children's literature is the foundation of a reading program, students must have many books. Ideally, there should be enough copies of the same book for each child to have his or her own copy for the duration of the book activities (a class set). Other times, enough copies of one book for a small group of students to use (a text set) will suffice.

We have already been able to accumulate many copies of various books, but we are always in need of more. If you would like to donate any children's books to our classroom collection, it would be greatly appreciated. There are a couple of ways that you can make such a donation.

- Donate books your family has already read (whether one or more).
- Purchase one copy, one text set (___ books), or even a class set (___ books) for the class at a local bookstore, used bookstore, or other vendor.

Although any book donation is of great help, below is a list of priority or preference books we need. Please let me know if you have any questions or comments. Thank you very much for your support and assistance.

Book Title	Author	Publication Info	Number of Copies Needed

Sincerely,

_____

© Carson-Dellosa

Story Summarizer

Question Creator

Imaginative Illustrator

Word Watcher

Bridge Builder

Circle Supervisor

Self Assessment

Name _____ Date _____

Book Title _____

Group Members _____

_____

Use this worksheet to assess yourself during literature circles. Circle your answer for each of the following statements. Then, explain your answer, if necessary. Be honest!

1. I finished the day's reading within the assigned time.   YES   NO
   If you circled no, explain why you did not finish. _____
   _____
   _____

2. I completed my role form to the best of my ability.   YES   NO
   If you circled no, explain why you did not complete the role form. _____
   _____
   _____

3. I talked about my role form with my group.   YES   NO
   If you circled no, explain why you did not talk about it. _____
   _____
   _____

4. I was a good listener.   YES   NO
   If you circled yes, list some of the things you did that made you a good listener. _____
   _____
   _____

   If you circled no, list some of the things you did that made you a not-so-good listener.
   _____
   _____
   _____

5. I used positive language during the discussion.   YES   NO
   Write some examples of positive language that you used or will use next time. _____
   _____
   _____
   _____

6. I did my very best.   YES   NO

Group Assessment

Name _____ Date _____

Book Title _____

Group Members _____

_____

Use this worksheet to assess your group during literature circles. Circle your answer for each of the following statements. Then, explain your answer, if necessary. Be honest!

1. My group worked well together.   YES NO
   If you circled yes, give some examples of how your group worked well together. _____

   _____

   _____

   If you circled no, give some examples of how your group did not work well together. _____

   _____

   _____

2. My group members completed the role forms to the best of their abilities.   YES NO
   If you circled no, explain. _____

   _____

   _____

3. My group shared and discussed our role forms.   YES NO
   If you circled no, explain why the group did not share and discuss, and write what the
   group could do better next time. _____

   _____

   _____

4. My group members were good listeners.   YES NO
   If you circled yes, list some of the things group members did that made them good listeners.

   _____

   _____

   If you circled no, list some of the things group members did that made them not-so-good
   listeners. _____

   _____

   _____

5. My group members used positive language during the discussion.   YES NO
   Write some examples of positive language that group members used or can use next time.

   _____

   _____

Name _____ Date _____

Book Title _____

Group Members _____

_____

Use this worksheet to assess yourself and your group members during literature circles. Circle your answer for each of the following statements. Be honest!

Myself

1. I finished the day's reading within the assigned time.   YES   NO

2. I completed my role form to the best of my ability.   YES   NO

3. I talked about my role form with my group.   YES   NO

4. I was a good listener. I made eye contact. I paid attention.
   I asked questions, and I did not interrupt.   YES   NO

5. I used positive language during the discussion.   YES   NO

6. I did my very best.   YES   NO

My Group Members

1. It seemed to me that my group members finished the day's reading.   YES   NO

2. All of my group members completed their role forms.   YES   NO

3. My group members talked about their role forms.   YES   NO

4. They were good listeners. They made eye contact. They paid attention.
   They asked questions, and they did not interrupt.   YES   NO

5. My group members used positive language during the discussion.   YES   NO

6. My group members seemed to do their very best.   YES   NO

Use the back of the paper to add any comments that you think are important for your teacher to know.

Name _____ Date _____

Book Title _____

Group Members _____

_____

Use this worksheet to highlight one literature circle group member who you feel did an outstanding job during literature circle time.

The Circle Star today is:

_____

Here are some reasons this person deserves to be the Circle Star.

_____

_____

_____

_____

_____

_____

_____

_____

_____

_____

_____

_____

_____

_____

Name _____ Date _____

This form will help us choose the books and groups for literature circles. Write your first choice (the book you would most like to read) next to #1, your second choice next to #2, etc. On the lines provided, write a short note about why you want (or do not want) to read each book.

Choice	Book Title	Reasons for wanting/not wanting to

1. _____   _____
   _____
   _____
   _____

2. _____   _____
   _____
   _____
   _____

3. _____   _____
   _____
   _____
   _____

4. _____   _____
   _____
   _____
   _____

5. _____   _____
   _____
   _____
   _____

Book and Theme Suggestions

This list is not comprehensive, but it does highlight many popular books teachers use for literature circles and other reading activities. Some books on this list are appropriate for older or more advanced readers, while others are perfect for younger or less accomplished readers. It is strongly suggested that you read any book that you or your students select, or at least have a good working knowledge of it *before* choosing it for students to read. When possible, the original publication information is included with the title and author, but there are many available editions of most of these books.

Single Books with Many Themes

Bridge to Terabithia by Katherine Paterson (Crowell, 1977).
(Themes: friendship, families, losing a friend, peer pressure, being different, poverty/economics)

Charlie and the Chocolate Factory by Roald Dahl (Knopf, 1964).
(Themes: bad habits, poverty/economics, integrity, fantasy)

Charlotte's Web by E. B. White (HarperCollins, 1952).
(Themes: friendship, animal stories, life cycles, science: spiders, growing up, losing a friend)

From the Mixed-up Files of Mrs. Basil E. Frankweiler by E. L. Konigsburg (Atheneum, 1967).
(Themes: running away, sibling relationships, mystery, family, city life, art)

Island of the Blue Dolphins by Scott O'Dell (Houghton Mifflin, 1960).
(Themes: survival, Native American life, self-sufficiency)

The Lion, the Witch and the Wardrobe by C. S. Lewis (HarperCollins, 1950).
(Themes: good versus evil, fantasy/science fiction, heroism, family, integrity)

Maniac Magee by Jerry Spinelli (Little, Brown, & Company, 1990).
(Themes: race relations, family, perseverance, friendship)

Summer of the Monkeys by Wilson Rawls (Doubleday, 1975).
(Themes: sibling relationships, science: monkeys, overcoming difficulties, perseverance)

Text Set Themes

Pets (Dogs)

Because of Winn-Dixie by Kate DiCamillo (Candlewick Press, 2000).
Hurry Home, Candy by Meindert DeJong (Harper & Row, 1953).
Old Yeller by Fred Gipson (HarperCollins, 1956).
Shiloh by Phyllis Reynolds Naylor (Atheneum, 1991).
Sounder by William Howard Armstrong (HarperCollins, 1969).
Stone Fox by John Reynolds Gardiner (Crowell, 1980).
Where the Red Fern Grows by Wilson Rawls (Doubleday, 1961).

Family Relationships

Any Ramona, Beezus, and Henry books by Beverly Cleary (Avon, Camelot, Harper Mass Market, HarperCollins, Scott Foresman, Trophy, etc.).
Bud, Not Buddy by Christopher Paul Curtis (Delacorte, 1999).
Sarah, Plain and Tall by Patricia MacLachlan (HarperCollins, 1985).
Stone Fox by John Reynolds Gardiner (Crowell, 1980).
Summer of the Monkeys by Wilson Rawls (Doubleday, 1975).

Book and Theme Suggestions

Historical Fiction
Catherine, Called Birdy by Karen Cushman (Clarion, 1994).
The Indian in the Cupboard by Lynne Reid Banks (Doubleday, 1981).
Little House on the Prairie by Laura Ingalls Wilder (Harper & Brothers, 1935).
Sarah, Plain and Tall by Patricia MacLachlan (HarperCollins, 1985).
The Sign of the Beaver by Elizabeth George Speare (Houghton Mifflin, 1983).
The Whipping Boy by Sid Fleischman (Greenwillow, 1986).

Fantasy/Science Fiction/Adventure
The Black Cauldron by Lloyd Alexander (Dell, 1965).
The Castle in the Attic by Elizabeth Winthrop (Holiday House, 1985).
The Chocolate Touch by Patrick Skene Catling (William Morrow, 1952).
The Indian in the Cupboard, Lynne Reid Banks (Doubleday, 1981).
James and the Giant Peach by Roald Dahl (Knopf, 1961).
Jumanji by Chris Van Allsburg (Houghton Mifflin, 1981).
The Lion, the Witch and the Wardrobe by C. S. Lewis (HarperCollins, 1950).
Mrs. Frisby and the Rats of NIMH by Robert C. O'Brien (Atheneum, 1972).
The Phantom Tollbooth by Norton Juster (Random House, 1964).
Tuck Everlasting by Natalie Babbitt (Farrar, Straus & Giroux, 1975).
A Wrinkle in Time by Madeleine L'Engle (Farrar, Straus & Giroux, 1962).

Life at School
The Best Christmas Pageant Ever by Barbara Robinson (HarperCollins, 1972).
The Best School Year Ever by Barbara Robinson (HarperCollins, 1994).
The Chalk Box Kid by Clyde Robert Bulla (Random House, 1987).
The Flunking of Joshua T. Bates by Susan Richards Shreve (Knopf, 1984).
Freckle Juice by Judy Blume (Dell, 1971).
Frindle by Andrew Clements (Simon & Schuster, 1996).
Harriet the Spy by Louise Fitzhugh (Harper & Row, 1964).
The Hundred Dresses by Eleanor Estes (Harcourt Brace, 1944).
There's a Boy in the Girls' Bathroom by Louis Sachar (Random House, 1988).

Wild Animals
The Missing 'Gator of Gumbo Limbo: An Ecological Mystery by Jean Craighead George (HarperCollins, 1991).
Mr. Popper's Penguins by Richard & Florence Atwater (Little, Brown & Company, 1938).
Owls in the Family by Farley Mowat (McLelland & Stewart, 1961).
Rascal: A Memoir of a Better Era by Sterling North (Penguin, 1984).
Summer of the Monkeys by Wilson Rawls (Doubleday, 1975).
The Wheel on the School by Meindert DeJong (Harper & Row, 1954).

Book and Theme Suggestions

Heroes and Heroines/Survival
Hatchet by Gary Paulsen (Bradbury, 1987).
Island of the Blue Dolphins by Scott O'Dell (Houghton Mifflin, 1960).
Maniac Magee by Jerry Spinelli (Little, Brown & Company, 1990).
Pippi Longstocking by Astrid Lindgren (Puffin, 1950).

Getting Along with People Who Are Different than Ourselves
The Cay by Theodore Taylor (Doubleday, 1969).
The Chalk Box Kid by Clyde Robert Bulla (Random House, 1987).
The Hundred Dresses by Eleanor Estes (Harcourt Brace, 1944).
Jennifer, Hecate, Macbeth, William McKinley, and Me, Elizabeth by E. L. Konigsburg (Atheneum, 1967).
Maniac Magee by Jerry Spinelli (Little, Brown & Company, 1990).

Challenging Society/Learning Tolerance
The Giver by Lois Lowry (Houghton Mifflin, 1993).
Maniac Magee by Jerry Spinelli, (Little, Brown & Company, 1990).
Number the Stars by Lois Lowry (Houghton Mifflin, 1989).
The View from Saturday by E. L. Konigsburg (Atheneum, 1996).

Series Children Enjoy

Books in a series offer a unique opportunity for children to grow up with characters, or to see them in different situations. For example, comparing Laura Ingalls as a child who resents her older sister, to Laura Ingalls as a teenager who describes sunsets in fantastic detail to the same sister who has become blind, can be a valuable lesson for children about how people and situations never remain the same.

Amber Brown series by Paula Danziger (Scholastic Paperbacks)
The Boxcar Children series by Gertrude Chandler Warner and others (Albert Whitman & Company)
Cam Jensen series by David Adler (Viking/Penguin/Putnam)
The Chronicals of Narnia by C. S. Lewis (HarperCollins)
Harry Potter series by J. K. Rowling (Scholastic Trade)
Horrible Harry series by Suzy Kline (Puffin/Viking/Kestral Press)
Judy Moody series by Megan McDonald (Candlewick Press)
Junie B. Jones series by Barbara Park (Random House Books for Young Readers)
Little House series by Laura Ingalls Wilder (HarperCollins)
Sideways Stories from Wayside School by Louis Sachar (Avon)

Authors Children Enjoy Who Have Written Several Books
(not necessarily in a series)

Judy Blume	Meindert DeJong	Louis Sachar
Roald Dahl	E. L. Konigsburg	E. B. White

Troubleshooting and FAQs

Now that you and your students are ready to make literature circles a regular part of your reading program, you may find that you stumble across some problems, challenges, and "technical difficulties." This chapter will answer most of your questions and provide possible solutions for some of those obstacles. Literature circles, like most other classroom activities, take planning and effort, but they can usually be adapted to your particular teaching situation. If you come across a problem which is not addressed here, take a step back and look at it as you would any other teaching situation.

▲▽▲▽▲▽▲▽▲▽▲▽▲▽▲▷

How do literature circles fit into my current reading program?

How literature circles fit into your current reading program will depend on your current framework and curriculum. Because curricular requirements vary

This Chapter Includes:

Answers to common questions addressing:

* how to work literature circles into a reading program

* how often to do literature circles

* adapting literature circles for all students

* occupying "early birds"

* reteaching students how to "do" literature circles

* troubleshooting for problem groups and individual students

* assessment and state tests

* presenting literature circles to administrators, colleagues, and parents

from state to state, and even school to school, you may have more limitations than other teachers. Or, you may have the freedom to "plug in" literature circles wherever and whenever you see fit. Determining how and where literature circles will fit in based on school requirements is the first step. For many teachers, the books they use for literature circles are at the core of their reading programs, so the circles blend in seamlessly as a supplement to their existing reading program. Other teachers build their reading programs around the books they and their students decide to use for literature circles. For example, let's say a class is reading *Ramona Quimby, Age 8* by Beverly Cleary (Scott Foresman, 1992). Four days of the week (or as many days as students do not do literature circles), the class would participate in other reading activities also based on *Ramona Quimby, Age 8*, such as holding a writing workshop, having taped read-aloud time, continuing daily phonics practice, etc. One of the reasons why it is simple to add literature circles to the regular list of activities in your reading classroom is that you can decide where and when they fit in.

How often should I do literature circles?

Some of the research on literature circles states that students should decide how many times groups will meet. If you feel that students are ready for this, then let them decide. However, letting students decide is not always desirable or even feasible in "real-world" classrooms. The frequency of meetings depends on many factors. One important factor to consider is the guidelines of your school's reading program. Restrictions and limitations vary greatly from state to state, and even from school to school. If you have the power to determine the frequency of literature circles, remember that they are not meant to be the sole component of your reading program, but they can be the main component. There are other skills, activities, and lessons you must incorporate in order to have an effective literature program. A good rule of thumb in the beginning is to have students meet for their circles approximately once a week. As students become more familiar with the routine and need less reteaching, you may decide to increase the number of sessions per week, because there will not be as much time devoted to reviewing the procedure.

If you are in a teaching situation that restricts your choice of activities, this may mean that you can only hold literature circle meetings once every two weeks, and not always on consecutive chapters. Or, you may be required to base the literature circle activities only on the required reading selection. Students will still benefit, however, from the discussion, the variation of roles and activities, and the book club atmosphere that literature circles provide.

How can I adapt literature circles for all students—regardless of their reading levels?

There are many ways to adapt literature circles to fit every student's needs. You know your students best, and you will use your professional judgment to decide what is best for your students. One of the ways to adapt the role forms for struggling readers is to simplify the forms. You can require fewer answers on the student role forms, or even better, make up your own forms to suit these students. Another way to help struggling readers is to pair them with a classmate so that they can "buddy-read" the day's selection and complete the role forms together. This "buddy" can be from the struggling reader's circle group or can be someone from another group who has the same role for the day (example: two Story Summarizers work together on their role forms). The latter is probably the better option because it enables two students to complete the same role, but present to different groups. Helping struggling readers is also an excellent opportunity for teacher-student one-on-one— *you* can be the struggling reader's buddy. Also, you will notice that the different forms for each role vary, and some may be more suitable for these readers. Keep this in mind when you make your role form assignments. Lastly, remember that even if these adjustments are not helpful, the setting of literature circles will automatically support the struggling reader. When the students join for their groups and discuss their roles, the other members will add their ideas and thoughts, so the struggling reader will be assisted by her circle members.

More proficient readers are challenged by the nature of literature circles because they naturally take on the roles of leaders. These students are the group members you will hear saying just what you hope to hear and igniting discussions within the circles. Additionally, these students can also serve as buddies for struggling readers. If a student does not seem challenged, even under these circumstances, then modify the role forms.

How can I occupy students who finish their reading or role forms faster than the rest of the class?

These "early birds" have a few options as to what to do while waiting for the rest of their group members. There are many enrichment activities that you can encourage students to do during this free time. The important thing is to keep them busy doing an activity related to the day's reading or current book. Familiarize students with whatever routine you choose before they begin, so that they will not interrupt the rest of the class while trying to figure out what to do and make everyone else take even longer.

First, instruct students who finish early to gather their literature circle materials (books, pencils, and role forms) and go to their preassigned group meeting locations. This serves as a signal to the other members that they are ready to begin discussing. Members who are still working on their role forms at their desks will make mental notes to speed up.

Next, as these early birds wait for their group members, they can reread the day's selection, read ahead, or review their role forms for errors and/or missing information. Many students will want to continue the reading; indeed, it may be difficult to stop them. Unless they are expected to make predictions as part of an assignment, students will benefit from reading the material more than once, so allow them to read ahead if possible.

Some students would rather do something else, so also consider giving them the option of doing something extra, such as highlighting vocabulary words in the book (or listing them on a sticky note if the book does not belong to the student), marking interesting sections with sticky notes, responding to the reading in a journal, etc.

Finally, refer to pages 73-76 for Early-Bird worksheets. These are designed to further enrich students' understanding of their reading. The Reader Response worksheet will help students explain their feelings about what they are reading. The Character Response worksheet will help students understand characterization by having them evaluate characters and think about which they would like to be, as well as letting them play author and change a few things. The Setting Response worksheet helps students think about places and times in which characters live. The Free Response worksheet allows students to express any feelings they have about the reading by responding to a short writing prompt. You may want to model the use of this worksheet, and show students how to dig up small but significant details. These worksheets can be also used for extra credit or homework.

How can I help a student who seems slow to finish reading assignments or role forms?

It is normal and expected that students will take different amounts of time to finish the reading and their role forms. This is due not only to the differences in student reading and writing abilities, but also the differences in the difficulty of the role forms. If a student is particularly slow at completing the role forms, first determine what is causing the delay. Is the student wasting time by being off task, or is he having trouble with the reading or role form? If the problem is caused by off-task behavior, use the usual management strategies to handle the situation. If the problem is due to the student's inability to work independently, pair him with a peer buddy or work one-on-one with him during the reading and role form completion. Remember that you can always adjust the role forms for struggling students. Finally, if you have a student who is not struggling, but is just a slower reader, consider allowing that student to complete a portion of each reading assignment for homework.

I followed the steps in Chapter 3 to train my students, but they just don't seem to " get it." What else can I do to help them understand?

Don't give up! As stated in Chapter 3, expect to see some glitches early on. It is probable that this type of interaction is new to students. The dialogue and discussion is usually what students have the most trouble getting used to, especially in the earlier grades. The first thing to do is observe and evaluate. Exactly what is it that students are not getting? Once you determine what areas students need assistance with, spend time reteaching these. It will be worth the extra time and effort required to review literature circles, because students will "get it," and begin to function independently in their groups.

Many students have difficulty executing the discussions required in the literature circles. Usually, the most effective way to handle this is to have students role-play again. You may decide to spend more time on this than you did originally to ensure that students understand what is expected. Start by restating what should occur within their groups. Remind them that although they should share what they answer on their role forms, the goal of literature circles is to get them to talk, discuss, even debate about their reading. Tell the class that these discussions should evolve naturally while they share their role forms and refer to the literature. Call several students to serve as volunteers, and role-play a literature circle meeting. Role-play along with students, perhaps serving as the Circle Supervisor, as well. Or, have students role-play while you direct and guide, providing specific feedback.

Additionally, consider conducting a question-and-answer session. A session like this will provide students with an opportunity to ask any and all questions and get clarity about any confusion. This will also help you determine what students are uncertain about. Often this is all that it takes for students to get the hang of it. Remember, they will get better with practice.

What can I do if the students are just "skimming," rather than discussing, the information on their role forms? How can I tell the difference?

Skimming most often occurs early on, when students are still not quite comfortable with the structure of literature circles. The best way to handle this is to remind them that they should share their ideas, not just read their role form answers. Sitting in and participating with the groups also helps because you can lead the discussion. If the groups have already met a few times, and they are still not getting involved in discussions and debates, you may want to take some time to reteach the concept. Explain what should occur within the groups and have the students role-play again, as you did in Chapter 3.

Here is an example of what skimming looks like for an Imaginative Illustrator.
"Here is the scene I visualized and drew, and this is what I wrote . . . ."

Here is an example of a student using the Imaginative Illustrator role form as a part of discussion.
"I visualized the part on page 42 when the author describes the setting and the character is really scared. See? I drew Johnny and his knees are shaking, and his eyes are really big, like he's scared. Then, I did the haunted house, with cobwebs, and it's really dark. And then I put these green squiggly things because the author says 'There was a strange, pungent odor that made Johnny feel sick.' Those were some of the words and sentences the author used that help me visualize this. Also, the author wrote 'The darkness closed in around him' and 'dusty webs hung from every corner.' I could see this all really clearly in my head. Which part did you visualize really clearly when you were reading?"

How can I tell if a group is not working together effectively?

Sometimes there are obvious signs that a group is not working together well. Unfortunately, there are other times when the signs are not so clear. The following are signs to watch for when identifying effectiveness and cooperation within a group.

Signs that a group is not working well:
- fights or arguments
- students' complaints to you
- groups who finish discussing significantly quicker than the allotted time
- groups who do not finish discussing within the allotted time
- students' assessment worksheets that indicate group problems
- one or more students who show reluctance to participate in literature groups (for example, asks to be excluded, prefers to work alone, or complains regularly)

What can I do if a group is not working together effectively?

The first thing you need to do is figure out *why* the group is not working together effectively. The best way to do this is to observe and monitor the group. Of course, if you sit in with the group, you may not see the problems that occur when you are not nearby. You may want to observe in a more subtle way—perhaps by sitting with another group so that you can overhear and watch. Did the students form this group? Is this perhaps a "clique" of friends that lends itself to bickering or social-izing instead of working? One student may be causing the problem, or it may be that the dynamics of this particular group just don't work.

Often when problems occur within the literature circles it is because there is some uncertainty among the members as to what they should do or say. This confusion can often lead to arguments. Therefore, it is imperative that you meet with the group and review the procedures, as well as try other strategies of reteaching.

If you have tried several strategies and the situation does not improve, you will have to make a decision. Do you divide these group members and go through the trouble of reorganizing the groups? This depends on how long these groups have been meeting. If students just started a book, and you really feel the best choice is to split up the group, it will be easier to do it early in the process than if the groups are midway through a book and have been meeting for weeks. Try to maintain the groups as they are, and simply monitor this group more closely than the others. You can accomplish this by sitting in with them more often or by taping their meetings when you are with other groups.

If all else fails, you can make the decision to split up the group and have these students work independently on the readings and role forms. Of course this is not ideal, because the purpose of literature circles is to have the students meet and discuss. Having them work independently means these students will be missing out on the most important component. However, students who are denied the group-meeting experience even once usually want to return to their groups and will negotiate with you for another chance. And, as a teacher who wants the students to benefit from this activity, you will be more than willing to come to an agreement.

I have a "problem student" who just isn't cooperating in the literature circle groups. I have tried everything! Should I exclude the student from the literature circles?

This is a difficult question, but one almost all teachers have to answer. You should treat this as you would any other situation involving a "problem student." Every "problem student" is different, and therefore warrants different considerations. First of all, assess whether you have really tried all options. Second, decide exactly *how* she isn't cooperating. Is she refusing to participate? If so, perhaps the student feels inadequate, unsure, or confused. Is she distracting other students in the group by engaging them in off-task behaviors? If so, try speaking to the group members privately and asking them to ignore the student unless she is on task. Is she participating incorrectly (completing the role forms the wrong way, not following directions, or speaking out of turn)? If so, perhaps she needs a review on literature circles. There are other general strategies you may want to attempt, as well. Consider assigning that student a "buddy" who will help her stay focused and on task. Work with the student one-on-one for a couple of weeks until you see some improvements. Have a private talk with the student to figure out why she is being uncooperative, and brainstorm some possible solutions together. Write up a teacher-student contract about acceptable behaviors.

If you have tried all of these things and nothing seems to work, then exclude the student from literature circles. This is especially important if she is constantly disrupting the rest of the class. Have the student do the same work as the rest of the class, except require her to do it independently and without the opportunity of sharing with the group. Ideally, once the student is excluded a couple of times, she will want to rejoin the group. When this occurs, allow her to return to the group under certain conditions and guidelines, so that the disruptive behavior does not happen again.

If the whole class is using one book, and there are no significant learning level issues, does it work better to give the same role forms to all of the groups? Or, should I still use different forms for each role?

This is a matter of personal preference. If all students are reading the same book, and they have similar reading levels, it is easier to use the same forms for everyone. Select the forms from each role that you would like to use, and then stick to those so everyone who is a Story Summarizer, for example, uses the same form. This makes teaching and reviewing the forms, comparing students' output, and record-keeping much simpler. If, however, some students would do better with certain forms, or if you prefer to add variety so students are exposed to different strategies, then use different forms at your discretion. You can also start out using one of the forms for each role and switch to a different form for the next book. For example, everyone uses #1 of each role for the first book, but for the second book you introduce and use #2 of each role.

How can I use literature circles for assessment purposes?

Not only can you assess the work done within literature circles for its own merit, you can also use students' work in literature circles to assess a variety of skills. There are a number of options in this area. The choice depends on your needs and assessment techniques. One easy way to assess skills is to create a rubric or checklist that includes the objectives you want students to master, such as comprehension, retelling, summarizing, vocabulary, etc., and then apply it to the role form that best demonstrates that skill. These rubrics may take a few moments to create, but will enable you to focus on very specific skills, and learn about areas in which students need improvement and practice. For example, the *Story-Summarizer* role forms are usually very indicative of the level of students' reading comprehension, so you could collect the *Story-Summarizer* forms and compare them to your rubric or checklist. You may decide to only assess a particular role for each student, or you may decide to grade all of them, or you could assess the same role for each group, which would give you a snapshot of how groups are performing on that skill.

Another type of assessment measures the cooperative behaviors exhibited in the circles. Create sheets for individual students or whole groups using the student-assessment worksheet (pages 56-59) as guides for your own. Then, fill out these forms while you are observing, participating, or watching/listening to recorded group meetings. Along with student-completed assessment forms, this type of assessment can help you troubleshoot any problems within groups and can help you decide how to group students for the next book.

How do literature circles help students prepare for state tests?

Research proves that literature circles improve reading comprehension, a major component of many required tests. Literature circles provide students with an opportunity to interact with literature and develop higher-order thinking skills. They must read independently and then demonstrate evidence of comprehension through filling out role forms and participating in group meetings. The role forms cover general, critical elements of literature study, as well as provide students with authentic opportunities to practice various reading strategies. Students become more aware of these reading strategies and use them to become more independent and active readers. There is research available on the benefits of incorporating literature circles into reading programs. (See page 9 and pages 78-79 for some available evidence.)

How can I prove to my principal/administrator that literature circles encourage learning, are not a waste of class time, and should be incorporated into my school curriculum?

There are a few ways you can convince your principal that literature circles are an effective use of instructional time. First, do research (see Chapter 5 for a list of resources) and provide your principal with some hard evidence that literature circles are, in fact, beneficial. Another option is to invite the principal to your class to observe literature circles in action. Surely, she will realize the advantages of literature circles once she sees your motivated and enthusiastic students reading, sharing, debating, interacting, and working. If inviting your principal to your class is not feasible, consider recording your students in their literature circles. Your principal can watch the video and ask any questions or voice any concerns. Once you have tried one or all of these tactics, your principal will probably see the benefits of literature circles.

How can I present and demonstrate literature circles to a group of parents or colleagues?

Usually, the most detailed and clear way to present literature circles to a group of adults is the same way in which you present it to students, especially if the group is not familiar with the concept. However, teachers rarely have time to get this intensive during a workshop. Regardless of your audience, the first step is to decide the purpose or goal of your presentation. Once you have identified the goal, the best means to present literature circles will be clear. Here are some general guidelines.

▶ If your goal is to **motivate fellow teachers** to implement literature circles in their own classrooms, one of the best ways to present the concept is to have them watch your students in action, either in person or on video.

▶ If your goal is to **show parents what your students do in class** (for parents' night, for example), showing them a video of their children in their circle discussion groups is also a great idea.

▶ If your goal is to **show off your students to administrators or other visitors**, have them come in and observe your class during literature circle time.

▶ If your goal is to **demonstrate (in a limited amount of time) how to implement literature circles to parents or teachers,** have them work in small groups to complete sample role forms using a literature excerpt from your class.

If you just want to introduce the idea to parents, send home the form letter on page 77. Remember, the more information parents have about their children's activities, the more likely they are to be helpful and supportive.

Early Bird Reader

▲ ▼ ▲ ▼ **Response Sheet**

Name _____ Date _____

Book Title _____

Group Members _____

_____

Use the following prompts to help you respond to the reading.

1. After reading pages _____ I feel _____ because

_____

_____

_____

2. My favorite character so far is _____ because _____

_____

_____

_____

3. The character I like least so far is _____ because _____

_____

_____

_____

4. My favorite part of the book so far is_____

_____

because_____

_____

_____

5. If I could change anything about the book so far, it would be _____

_____

_____

_____

_____

Early Bird Character

▲ ▼ ▲ ▼ **Response Sheet**

Name _____ Date _____

Book Title _____

Group Members _____

_____

Use the following prompts to help you think about the characters and respond to the reading.

1. My favorite character so far is _____ because _____

_____
_____
_____
_____

2. The character I like least so far is _____ because _____

_____
_____
_____
_____

3. If I could be any character from the book, I would be _____ because

_____
_____
_____
_____

4. If I could change any character from the book in any way, I would change _____
by _____

_____
_____
_____

The reason I would change this character is because _____

_____
_____
_____
_____
_____

Early Bird Setting

▲ ▼ ▲ ▼ **Response Sheet**

Name _____ Date _____

Book Title _____

Group Members _____

_____

Use the following prompts to help you think about the setting and respond to the reading.

1. Time: I think this story takes place _____ because _____

_____

_____

_____

_____

2. What are other events that could have happened/did happen during this time period?

_____

_____

_____

_____

3. Place: I think this story takes place _____ because _____

_____

_____

_____

_____

4. List facts you know about the place/places where the action in the story occurs.

_____

_____

_____

_____

5. List descriptive words and phrases from the book that help you identify the time and place from the story. _____

_____

_____

_____

▲ ▼ ▲ ▼ Response Sheet

Name _____ Date _____

Book Title _____

Group Members _____

_____

Use this worksheet to respond to the reading. You may respond to one or more of the following prompts, or you can create your own writing prompt. Use the lines below and the back of this sheet or more paper if you need it.

Reading Response Prompts

- I did not like the part when . . .
- I felt excited when . . .
- I don't understand why . . .
- I felt happy when . . .
- I felt sad when . . .
- I think that . . .
- I noticed that . . .

- I felt angry when . . .
- I felt worried when . . .
- I liked the part when . . .
- I was confused when I read the part about . . .
- I know how the character _____ felt when . . .
- A question I have is . . .

_____

_____

_____

_____

_____

_____

_____

_____

_____

_____

_____

Dear Parents/Family,

Research shows that quality literature should be the core of any good reading program. Therefore, we will be using children's books as part of our classroom reading curriculum. One of our most exciting literature-based activities will be literature circles. Literature circles are groups of approximately five students that gather on a regular basis to discuss the book(s) they are reading in class. The purpose of literature circles is to get students to think about, discuss, and even debate on quality literature.

I want to share with you how this new and exciting program works in our classroom. Here is a basic overview. This should help you understand what your child is doing as part of his or her literature instruction.

- The first steps include assigning literature circle groups and selecting the books. Every day that we do literature circles, each student has a different role or job.
- On a literature circle day, students read the day's selection independently (this can be a chapter or a few pages), and then complete their role forms. The purpose of role forms is to get students to interact with the literature. The role forms require students to complete activities such as creating and answering questions for the day's reading, illustrating particular scenes, writing journal-type entries on what they read, or finding and working with vocabulary words.
- Then, the circle groups meet with their books and completed role forms in hand. They discuss, ask questions, and sometimes debate what they've just read using their role forms as guides.
- After the group discussion, we reconvene as a class and talk about what happened in the literature circles.

There are many benefits to literature circles, such as:
- Students read and think about quality literature.
- Students are motivated by the group work.
- Each day, students complete different role forms, so they don't get bored.
- The reading and discussion simulates "real-life" reading and book discussion, just like a book club for adults. (Imagine yourself reading the latest best-seller and then talking to your friends about it.)
- It improves reading comprehension and vocabulary.
- It's fun!

I encourage you to ask your child about this exciting and new reading activity. Feel free to contact me with any questions, comments, or suggestions.

Sincerely,

_____

Resources and Bibliography

In the early 1980s, teachers like Karen Smith in Phoenix, Arizona, helped to start the literature circles "movement." Her group of students found a box of book sets, requested to borrow them, and formed their own book club discussions that were similar to book clubs for adults. Other teachers learned from these early experiments that students function well when they choose their own literature and monitor their own progress.

Since literature circles began, many scholars have researched, studied, and implemented this approach to teaching literature. The concept of literature circles has spread through presentations and articles by experts, theorists, and educators. The concept has also spread through the grassroots efforts of teachers who wanted to share with their colleagues this unique approach to teaching literature. Consult the following resources to learn more about the origins, benefits, and practices of literature circles.

Bibliography

Daniels, Harvey. *Literature Circles: Voice and Choice in the Student-Centered Classroom*. York, Maine: Stenhouse Publishers, 1994.

Hollingsworth, Liz. "Literature Circles Spark Interest." *Schools in the Middle* 8:2 (1998): 30-3.

Raphael, Taffy E. "Teaching question answer relationships, revisited." *The Reading Teacher* 39 (1986): 516-522.

Rosenblatt, Louise. M. *The Reader, the Text, the Poem: The Transactional Theory of the Literary Work*. Carbondale, IL: Southern Illinois University Press, 1978.

Samway, Kathering Davies, and Gail Whang. *Literature Study Circles in a Multicultural Classroom*. York, Maine: Stenhouse Publishers, 1996.

Samway, Kathering Davies, G. Whang, C. Cade, M. Gamil, M. A. Lubandina, and K. Phommachanh. "Reading the Skeleton, the Heart, and the Brain of a Book: Students' Perspectives on Literature Study Circles." *The Reading Teacher* 45:3 (1991): 196-205.

Santa, Carol, Lynn T. Havens, and Evelyn M. Maycumber. *Project CRISS: Creating Independence through Student-owned Strategies.* Montana: Kendall Hunt Publishing Company, 1996.

Short, Kathy G., and Kathryn M. Pierce, eds. *Talking About Books: Creating Literate Communities.* Portsmouth, NH: Heinemann, 1990.

Tompkins, Gail E. *50 Literacy Strategies: Step by Step.* New Jersey: Merrill, 1998.

Notes